Seasons Around You

Autumn

Saviour Pirotta

WAYLAND

Seasons Around You

 Autumn

 Spring

Summer

Winter

Cover photograph: Playing in autumn leaves.

Title page: Trick or treating at Hallowe'en.

Produced for Wayland Publishers Limited by
Roger Coote Publishing
Gissing's Farm, Fressingfield
Eye, Suffolk IP21 5SH, England

Series designer: Jan Stirling
Book designer: Victoria Webb

First published in 1998 by
Wayland Publishers Ltd
61 Western Road, Hove
East Sussex BN3 1JD, England

Find Wayland on the Internet at http://www.wayland.co.uk

British Library Cataloguing in Publication Data
Pirotta, Saviour, 1958–
   Autumn. – (Seasons around you)
   1. Autumn – Pictorial works – Juvenile literature
   I. Title
   508.2

ISBN 0 7502 2278 6

Printed and bound by EuroGrafica, Vicenza, Italy.

Picture acknowledgements
Bubbles 13, 18; Eye Ubiquitous 6 (Paul Seheult), 17
(Skjold); FLPA 9 (Roger Wilmshurst), 11 (Roger
Wilmshurst), 19 (JM Fichaux/Sunset), 20 (J Watkins), 21
(Roger Wilmshurst); Getty Images *Cover* (Dale Durfee),
12 (Dale Durfee), 15 (FLPA), 25 (Wayne Eastep); Hong
Kong Tourist Association 28; Hutchison Library 26 (Liba
Taylor); Image Bank 7 (Jeff Smith); Impact 14 (Charles
Worthington), 29 (Jeremy Nicholl); Papilio 10 (Jamie
Harron); J Allan Cash 24; Skjold 23; Wayland Picture
Library 5, 16 (Tim Woodcock); TWP/Tim Woodcock 4;
Zefa 8 (Gollnow), 22, 27 (F Paul).

Contents

Words that appear in **bold** are explained in the glossary on page 32.

Goodbye summer

What do you notice at the beginning of autumn? The weather gets colder and the days get shorter.

We put away our summer clothes.
We need thicker clothes now.
Sometimes we need **waterproofs.**

Back to school

The summer holidays are over.
Children go back to school.

It's the start of another school year.
Everyone is in a new class, with
a new teacher.

Birds in autumn

Swallows fly south in search of food and warm weather.

The birds that stay behind eat lots of autumn berries to get fatter. Their fat will keep them warm in the winter.

Animal life

Hedgehogs **hibernate** in the winter. Before they go to sleep, they eat as much as they can to get fatter.

Squirrels store nuts close to their nests.
They'll need them when it's too cold to
look for food.

Falling leaves

The leaves on trees turn yellow, orange and brown. Then they fall to the ground.

Now is the time to plant bulbs that
will grow next spring – crocuses,
daffodils and tulips.

13

Autumn on the farm

It's time to gather the last **harvests** of the year – apples, pears and berries.

Farmers **plough** their fields.
They plant seeds such as wheat,
which they can harvest next summer.

Harvest festivals

At school and in church we give thanks for the harvests. Everyone brings food for this special celebration.

In North America, people celebrate
Thanksgiving with a special feast.
They thank God for being generous.

Autumn food

It's nice to have hot, filling food when it's cold. We eat stew, soup and hot apple pie.

Sometimes you can buy roasted chestnuts
in the street and eat them while they're hot.

Seeds and games

Some trees scatter their seeds on the ground. The seeds will open up in spring, when the weather is warmer.

Conkers are horse chestnut seeds.
They are great fun to play with.

Hallowe'en

The greengrocer sells large pumpkins.
They are hollowed out to make spooky
Hallowe'en lanterns.

Ding dong! The doorbell rings.

It's children, trick or treating.

Trick or treat? A scare or a sweet?

23

Guy Fawkes Night

Penny for the Guy! Penny for the Guy! These children are collecting money to buy fireworks.

On **Guy Fawkes** Night, crowds gather around bonfires. Fireworks whizz and bang. They fill the night with colour.

25

Rosh Hashanah

Rosh Hashanah is the start of the
Jewish New Year. People eat sweet
foods to make the coming year sweet.

In the temple, a man blows the shofar.
It is a musical instrument made from
a ram's horn.

Other festivals

In autumn, Chinese people celebrate the **Moon Festival**. They buy lanterns and eat special cakes, called moon cakes.

In Hindu and Sikh homes, Divali is the festival of light. Lamps are lit to show that good triumphs over evil.

Autumn activities

GEOGRAPHY

Comparing localities Using a globe or an atlas, chart the progress of a swallow as it flies to Africa. Why do you think it is going there? What is the difference between winter at home and winter in Africa?

Effects of weather Which animals in this book are preparing to hibernate in the winter? Draw pictures of their hideouts.

Make a list of the activities you do in the summer. Make another list of what you do in autumn. Why do you do some things in one season and not in another? How many of these changes are due to the weather?

DESIGN AND TECHNOLOGY

Design and make a tool that could be used at harvest time on a farm.

ENGLISH

Write a poem or short story about autumn.

Write down the alphabet and alongside each letter, write a word beginning with that letter, linked in some way to autumn.

DANCE AND DRAMA

Find one of the many stories about the Chinese Moon Festival and act it out in a short play. You could use Chinese masks to portray the various characters.

Create an Indian dance showing the story of Rama and Sita. Use sitar music in the background.

Improvize the movement of leaves falling off trees and being blown about by the wind. Where will they end up?

SCIENCE

Light and dark Sow two beans in plastic cups (one in each cup). Put one cup in a dark box with holes for aeration. Put the other in a warm, well-lit place. Which of the beans grows best?

Making and detecting sounds Make a list of as many autumn sounds as you can, for example, crunching leaves, geese flying overhead. How do the calls differ? Do the biggest birds make the loudest sounds? Do the smallest produce the tiniest sounds?

Grouping materials Collect leaves from evergreen and deciduous trees (leaves that have turned brown) and sort them into two groups. Why do the deciduous leaves turn brown, whereas the evergreen leaves stay green?

Changing materials Make drawings of your school grounds in autumn and in summer. What differences do you notice between the two drawings? What effect has the season had?

MATHS

Compare the hours of daylight on 20 October with those on 20 June. Calculate the difference. How does this affect your daily life?

Compare the shapes, sizes and colours of various fallen leaves.

RE

Make Divali cards to exchange with friends.

Write poems thanking God for the harvest. It is said that Lakshmi, the goddess of wealth, visits clean, well-lit houses. Get into groups and tidy your classroom. Then light candles and invite Lakshmi to bestow her blessings on all the class.

Topic web

MUSIC	ART	DANCE AND DRAMA
Autumn sounds	Making pictures with seeds	Dance of the Falling Leaves
	Making camouflage masks	Story of Hallowe'en
		Ghost stories
		Playing the shofar

SCIENCE
Light and heat
Day and night
Autumn sounds
Animals in autumn
Growth of plants
Seeds
Recognize different leaves,
  seeds and flowers
Autumn colours and materials

AUTUMN TOPIC WEB

GEOGRAPHY
Farm and city
The four seasons
Changing environment
Attractive and unattractive
  environments
Effects of weather on people
  and their surroundings
Autumn food
Autumn clothes

MATHS
Measuring and comparing
  hours of daylight
Measuring rainfall
Leaf shapes and patterns
Sequence of seasons

RE
Thanksgiving
Moon Festival
Harvest Festival
Rosh Hashanah
Divali

ENGLISH
Importance of
  correct sequence

HISTORY
Guy Fawkes Night
Hallowe'en
Harvest

Resources

NON-FICTION
Autumn Festivals by H. Bliss (Watts, 1995)

Autumn on the Farm by Janet Fitzgerald
(Evans, 1995)

Clothes in Hot and Cold Places by Simon Crisp
(Wayland, 1996)

Divali by Kerena Marchant (Wayland, 1996)

Harvest Festival by Clare Chandler
(Wayland, 1997)

Life Stories: Guy Fawkes by Clare Chandler
(Wayland, 1995)

The Seasons by Debbie MacKinnon
(Frances Lincoln, 1995)

Weather Facts by P. Eden and C. Twist
(Dorling Kindersley, 1995)

Seasonal Crafts: Autumn by Gillian Chapman
(Wayland, 1997)

FICTION AND POETRY
Autumn Story by Jill Barklem (Collins Brambly
Hedge series, 1980). The adventures of the mice
of Brambly Hedge, with illustrations showing the
countryside in Autumn.

Poems for Autumn by Robert Hull (Wayland, 1995).
Seasonal poems from around the world, illustrated
with colour photographs.

Glossary

Divali The Hindu festival of light.

Guy Fawkes A man who tried to blow up the English Houses of Parliament on 5 November, 1605. On 5 November every year, people in Britain light bonfires and burn models of Guy Fawkes, called 'Guys', to celebrate the fact that he failed.

Hallowe'en An ancient festival from Europe, which started by people remembering friends and people in their family who had died.

Harvests Times of the year when ripe crops are gathered.

Hibernate To sleep through the winter.

Moon Festival A Chinese festival, which celebrates a successful harvest.

Plough Break up the soil in fields, usually soon after the crops have been harvested.

Swallows Small birds, which fly south for the autumn and winter, to reach countries that are warmer at those times of year.

Thanksgiving An American or Canadian harvest festival.

Waterproofs Clothes that keep you dry. They are made from a material that does not let water through.

Index